The Works of a Free Soul
A poetry Collection

Stephanie Jeanty

Copyright ©2018 Stephanie Jeanty

The Works of a Free Soul

Manufactured in the UNITED STATES of AMERICA

ISBN: 978-1732250802

All rights reserved. No parts of this publication The Works of a Free Soul may be reproduced, disturbed, or transmitted in any form or by any means, or sold without the author's permission.

First Edition April 2018

Self-Publishing by Stephanie Jeanty

Contents

Author's Note

ONE   Tales of Love.. 3

Two   Tales of Heartbreak &Pain...................................... 22

Three   Tales of Freedom... 41

Four   Tales of Hope.. 46

Acknowledgements

Author's Note

I have been writing poems from a young age to express myself. Through the power of words my thoughts and my feelings have come to life. I am nervous and excited to share this collection of poetry with you. It was tough deciding to share my passion with you because these pieces are some of the raw thoughts, emotions and feelings that come from within me. I realized it's now or never to let other's share a part of my gift.

As you read each piece of work, my hope is that it will resonate with you. I hope each piece of work will take you on a journey of love, hope, heartbreak, pain and freedom. I appreciate you taking the time to read this collection of my work.

- Stephanie Jeanty, 2018

Tales of Love

Boyfriend and Girlfriend

Boyfriend & Girlfriend

Hand in Hand

Along the seashore

In the moonlight

Their steps in rhythm

with the sea breeze

They look

up at the same star twinkling

Hear

the same sound of waves dancing

Look into each other's eyes

with the same intensity

Their arms sway

with the same movement

Their movement slow in beat

They keep walking in beat

The warmth of one

touching

The warmth of the other

The love within one

reaching out for the other

And the pain of one

knowing

the pain of the other

Along the seashore

In the moonlight

Boyfriend and Girlfriend

Hand in Hand

One special night

One special night

A kiss to die for

A touch that sends chills down my body

The soft smell of your cologne

Battling the sweet smell of my perfume

A soft whisper that makes me feel like nothing else matters

Words that we share alone

The brushing of your body against mine

Causing me to feel lifeless

A night not like others

Untitled

Your lips to my lips creates a drunken ecstasy

through my body

The feeling of everlasting bliss dances upon

my lips

Your hands frolic with my hands in a

rhythmic way

Bliss

Bliss travels through the soul

Hands touch velvet skin

Roses- Kiss of life

Ecstasy

Ecstasy pours through

The look in your eyes drives me insane

Your touch lasts forever

Your kiss, feeling of highness

I try to fight the feeling

Untitled

An angel on earth

A blessing in disguise

The beholder of my heart

Protector from all danger

Reason for my aspirations

Inspiration for who I am today

Love of my life that God has blessed me with

Before

Before I fell in love

I never knew what real love was

Thought love wasn't meant for me

But one unexpected day that all changed

That day you brought the sun into my life

You took all the pain away

Open my eyes to all the truths of life

Showed me inner beauty is stronger than outer beauty

Proved to me that I can love openly again despite the pains of the past

Dear Future Husband

I imagine how we'll meet

I envision how we'll be friends before lovers

We will complement each other's calling not complicate it

We will be one

We will speak into each other's purpose

We will pray and intercede on each other's behalf

We'll love kindly, we will love with patience

We'll build together

We'll never sleep with anger towards each other

I'll submit to you as the leader of our family without fearing submission

I'll sow into your purpose

I'll never break you

I'll uplift

I'll cover you

As the Word says "I'll be the bone of your bone, the flesh of your flesh"

You'll have revelation of who I am

You'll lead our family with vision

You'll cover me

You'll protect me

This is my letter to you

All because of love

You asked me if I'm ready

I act like I don't know what you're talking about

Again, you asked me if I am ready to take the next step in our relationship

I reply yes

But deep down I'm not sure

It's just that I don't want you to leave

I know I'm probably going to be making the greatest mistake in my life

But I'm willing to do it for you

Cause I love you

You think

You think I don't care

You think I don't like you

You think I'd rather be with him

You think I am just playing games with you

You think there's something wrong with you

You think you're not good enough for me

But it's not you, it's me

My feelings for you scare me

Lets

Let's be together

Let's just forget about the past

Let's just see how things go

Let's just stay in each other arms

Let's look at the night stars

Let's just be with each other forever

You want....

Us to be closer

To be an item

Us to be serious

Us to make more promises

Us to share a special moment

Us to last forever

To do everything that you think will make me happy

But what about what I want?

Can you show me the way?

Can you show me the way and guide me?

To that place where no one else can take me

A place that is so serene that no one knows we're there

Only sound that can be heard is the soft baby like whimpers, I let out as you explore

Take me farther and farther into our own private world

Please Baby, don't resist

Cause all my guards are down

Just explore and live

Someone Special

He's my shining armor

He's my night and day

He's the light of my life

He's the stars that twinkles in my sky

When my rainy day comes along he makes me smile

Love

Love is a feeling that's everlasting

Love is what you feel in your heart

Love is something all people experience

Love is a strong feeling

Love is a feeling that will never die

Love is what brings two people together

Quest for love

What is this thing called love?

Is it forever?

Worth looking for?

Something you can count on?

Do you receive or give love?

Is it mandatory to have love?

Where can you search for it?

Does it come from the heart?

Is it the basis of life?

Can you live without it?

Does everybody find love?

Is it simple to find?

Can it be right in front of you?

Is worth dying for?

Is it a real feeling or a spoken word that everyone says?

I guess it's a never-ending quest

He…….

Holds me when I need him to

Wipes the tears from my eyes

Takes me to places I've never been to before

Takes my hand and guides me

Whispers sweet words into my ear as we dance the night away

Caresses my cheek with the gentle stroke of his hand

His kisses fill my empty vessels

Tales of Heart Break

&

Pain

Cheater

There's a saying "once a cheater always a cheater"

We've been together for the past 2 years

But I know there's something going on

Why are you doing this to me?

I gave you my heart and you are breaking it

Your return

Somewhere out there I know I'll find you

When I find you the sun will shine once more

However, you're not here

So, there's only dark days

Days I wish would brighten up

A love that's unconditional is now gone

And left with a heart of pain

Where are you?

Why did you leave?

Why have you made my days dark?

But I have hope one day you'll return

What if....

I said no instead of yes

We did not get so close

I said I was not in love with you

I wasn't so serious about you

We were just friends with benefits

Would we still be together?

I Thought....

I found my better half

I was in love

You would be here till the end

Your feelings were as strong as mine

I was the one that fulfilled your needs

I would be the one you would come home to every night

I was your baby girl

What happened?

What happened to us?

We had sex

I got pregnant

You said the baby wasn't yours

I am taking care of our sons now by myself

You don't even come see them

You see me in the streets with them, you go the other way

When I walk by you in school, you call me ho, slut and trick

I laugh it off

Boy, you left me out in the cold

What happened? You were supposed to be there

Help me live

I have no food

I'm hungry

I'm alone

My parents have died of AIDS

There's no one here protecting me but me

Last night the mean men came and raped me

It's now 6 months later and I'm feeling very sick

I go to the medicine man, he says I have AIDS

I'm dying

Help me live

Homage to Haiti

Haiti, our hearts are breaking

There's a lot of people dying

Tears are endless

Hunger is killing

Poverty is rising

Kidnapping is happening

Normal life no longer exists

Fear is now the normal life

When will the tears stop?

When will there be no more fear?

Love story

Been together for two years

Shared things with you that I wouldn't share with just anyone

Told you my deepest and darkest secrets

Committed myself to you

Picked you up when you were down

Alienated my friends for you

Lost who I was for you

Forgot what normal life was like

Loved you more than life itself

And now baby you are telling me that you want to give up

Guess you got to go then

I give up too

Trials of Love

Love, where have you gone?

Did you fly away like a bird?

Slip through my hands unnoticed

Love, did you decide to walk away like nothing happened?

Love, did you know without you the sun does not rise?

Love, you're the reason my tears flow endlessly like a river

Darkness

Darkness lives inside thee

Thoughts of dying haunts your mind daily

But you push them out

Fear

A look of nervousness

Fear that you are no longer pure

Cause that man hurt you

I have...

I have no food

I have no clothes

No mother and father to look after me

No home to go to

No love to look forward to

The streets are my home

The kind strangers are my parents

An existence without an existence

Do you even know I exist?

Guess you don't

Because you would've proven it

What do I have to do so you can know I exist?

Do I have to change the way I look?

Change into something I'm not

However, I am not going to do these things

But it hurts you don't pay attention to my mere existence

Heartbreak

Feel trap in a web of despair

Loneliness that's overwhelming

Pain that's overbearing to carry

Constant tears, that are inconsolable

Darkness of unforgiveness

Loss of being

Rain of tears that never end

Full heart of sadness

Constant wondering and thinking of how things could have been

Loss of Love

Stuck in a dark hole without light

Why can't this pain end?

Missing You

Feels like my world has been turned upside down

Feels like there's nothing to live for

I cry the night away

The pain is ripping through my heart

No greater importance left in life

Thinking about how things were

Hoping faith will bring us together again

Cause I'm missing you

Losing you

I'm losing you

I'm losing your trust

The love is slowly disappearing

I can't longer call you my knight and shining armor

I'm losing that special light that shines for me

But I can't stand to lose you

Cause my world will become dark

You left me

With tears in my eyes

Sorrow in my heart

Hurt beyond hurt

A constant reminder of togetherness

Memories of happiness between two people

Hope that someday we'll meet again

The dignity that will help me be strong

Am I disease?

Am I disease?

You see me you run away

I come near, you back away

Ask you for things, you're afraid to give it to me

You talk to your friends about how icky I am

Ask for your friendship and you look like you just saw an alien

Try to talk to you but you ignore me

But if it is someone else

You give them your undivided attention

Tales of Freedom

Accept me

Accept me for who I am

Accept me as an individual

Accept me as any other girl

Accept me for who I am

Accept me for my specialties

But not for my looks

Symbols

What are symbols?

Symbols are expressions

Symbols are things expressed in many ways

A symbol can represent life and death

A symbol shows happiness and sadness

A symbol is me, a person

Many people can't understand my symbolism

Because I'm a different symbol

A symbol that's indifferent is me

That's what God wanted me to be

Me as an individual

There's a lot you don't know about me

You just think I'm an average girl

I may look like I'm an average girl

However, there's something that sets me apart from those average girls

And that's my uniqueness

This helps me be the smart and beautiful person I am

I Dance Because

I dance because it frees my soul

It transports me to this new world

It unifies my soul

An escape from the problems

Relaxation from stress

A time to be myself

Way to express myself

It makes me feel like a spiritual being

Make me feel pure as a white dove

But it's about time for me to dance my way to a newer place of being

Tales of Hope

Loss soul

I've walked in a valley of dark shadows

There seems to be no light to guide me

I have fallen into that valley of dark shadows

There is no escape route to this endless pain

But the Lord will be my light and guide me through the valley of dark shadows

In despair

I may walk in a shadow of distress

May I become weak with despair or distress?

Even when I'm heartbroken with despair or distress

There is something miraculous that happens

It may be the light of the Lord

That's showing me the way to go or I will lay to rest with peace in my soul without distress or despair

Acknowledgements

First and foremost, I thank God for giving me the courage and the strength to go on this journey of putting my writing in print. I know without God, I would not have the courage to share my pieces with the world. I thank God for giving me the passion to write. I am grateful for the path that the poets, writers and authors before made for me so that my own dream of being an author could be realized.

Thank you to everyone that has always encouraged to believe in myself and in my work as well. Without your encouragement, this could not be possible. I love you all.

www.ingramcontent.com/pod-product-compliance
Lightning Source LLC
Chambersburg PA
CBHW081354040426
42450CB00016B/3438